Timber
Many Uses

Trees

This is a garden.

The garden has trees.

This is a **forest.**

The forest has trees too.

The trees in the forest will be cut down.

Logs

Look at the trees.
The trees will be
cut into **logs.**

Wood

Look at the logs. The logs will be cut into **wood.**

My plane is made
from wood.

This house is made from wood.

This swing is made from wood.

Recycling wood

We can **recycle** wood.

13

We can recycle
this wood.

We can recycle
this wood.

Glossary

forest

logs

recycle

wood